WORKBOOK

For

THE GARDEN WITHIN

Where the War with Your Emotions End and Your Most Powerful Life Begins

David Prints

This companion workbook is designed to enhance your reading experience and provide additional exercises, activities, and supplementary material to further support the concepts presented in the original book.

Table Of Content

How to Use This Workbook..4

Summary...6

The Seedling... 8

    key Lessons...................................... 8

    Self-Reflection Questions....................... 10

    Check The Flow................................ 16

    Key Lessons......................................16

    Self- Reflection Questions...................... 18

Good Ground and Your Most Powerful Life........................ 23

    Key Lessons......................................23

    Self-Reflection Questions....................... 25

Ground Zero..30

    Key Lessons......................................30

    Self-Reflection Questions....................... 32

How Does Your Garden Grow?.....................................37

    Key Lessons......................................37

    Self-Reflection Questions....................... 39

Water,Water Everywhere...44

    Key Lessons......................................44

    Self-Reflection Questions....................... 46

Dust of the Ground..51

    Key Lessons......................................51

Self-Reflection Questions.................................... 53

Shaky Ground.. **58**

Key Lessons..58

Self-Reflection Questions.................................... 60

Wilderness...**65**

Key Lessons..65

Self-Reflection Questions.................................... 67

The Wisdom of Trees...**72**

Key Lessons..72

Self-Reflection Questions.................................... 74

A Tree in the Temple..79

Key Lessons..79

Self-Reflection Questions.................................... 81

Healing the Broken Heart.. **87**

Key Lessons..87

Self- Reflection Questions................................... 89

Self-Assessment Questions.................................... **94**

How to Use This Workbook

Welcome to the companion workbook for the book you have chosen. This section will provide you with valuable guidance on how to maximize the benefits of using this companion workbook to complement your reading of the original book.

To ensure a smooth transition into the workbook, a concise summary of the key points covered in the original book is provided. This summary aims to refresh your memory and prepare you for the in-depth exploration of the key lessons and self-reflection questions in each chapter.

Each chapter in this companion workbook corresponds to a chapter in the original book. Within each chapter, you will find key lessons extracted from the original book, followed by thought-provoking self-reflection questions. These questions are designed to help you internalize the teachings, apply them to your life, and gain deeper insights into the subject matter.

Towards the end of the workbook, you will encounter a section dedicated to self-evaluation questions. These questions are carefully crafted to encourage introspection and assess your understanding of the material presented in both the original book and this companion workbook. Take your time and answer them thoughtfully to track your progress and growth.

Summary

"The Garden Within: Where the War with Your Emotions Ends and Your Most Powerful Life Begins" by Dr. Anita Phillips is a transformative and insightful book that challenges conventional beliefs about emotions and offers a path to harnessing their power for a more fulfilling life.

Dr. Anita Phillips, a trauma therapist and mental health expert, begins by debunking the common misconception that emotions are our enemies. Instead, she asserts that emotions are not meant to be suppressed, managed, or mastered. They are essential aspects of our human experience, and when embraced, they can become powerful allies on our journey to self-discovery and personal growth.

The book draws a compelling analogy between the human heart and a garden. Just as gardens thrive in fertile soil, the abundant life we all seek can only be cultivated in the soil of our hearts. Dr. Phillips blends elements of faith, the latest findings in neurobiology, and her extensive experience as a licensed therapist to guide readers on this transformative journey.

The Seedling

key Lessons

1.Nurturing Your Emotions: Emotions are like fragile seedlings that need care and attention to thrive. Just as you tend to a garden, you must nurture your emotions to grow in a healthy way.

2.Roots of Understanding: To understand and work with your emotions, you need to dig deep, like examining the roots of a plant. Explore the origins of your emotions and their connections to your past experiences.

3.Acceptance and Growth: Embracing your emotions is the first step toward growth. Just as a seedling must be accepted as it is, you should accept your emotions without judgment or suppression.

4.Pruning for Strength: Like pruning a plant for better growth, you can learn to manage and guide your emotions constructively. This involves acknowledging when certain emotions need to be trimmed or redirected.

5.Watering Your Soul: Your emotional well-being requires nourishment, just like a plant needs water. Consider what activities and practices "water" your soul, providing sustenance for your emotional growth.

6.Patience and Persistence: Cultivating emotional well-being takes time and effort, much like tending to a garden. Be patient with yourself and persist in your journey to understand and embrace your emotions.

Self-Reflection Questions

1.How can you nurture your emotions in a way that allows them to grow and flourish?

_____

_____

_____

_____

_____

_____

_____

_____

_____

2.Have you ever explored the roots of your emotions, seeking to understand their origins and significance in your life?

_____

_____

_____

_____

_____

_____

_____

_____

3.Can you think of a recent situation where you accepted your emotions without judgment? What was the outcome?

_____

_____

_____

_____

_____

_____

_____

_____

_____

4.Are there any specific emotions in your life that may need pruning or redirection for your personal growth?

_____

_____

_____

_____

_____

_____

_____

_____

_____

_____

5.What practices or activities provide nourishment for your emotional well-being, similar to watering a plant?

_____

_____

_____

_____

_____

_____

_____

_____

_____

6.In what ways can you practice patience and persistence in your journey to cultivate emotional well-being, knowing that it takes time and effort?

_____

_____

_____

_____

_____

_____

_____

Check The Flow

Key Lessons

1.Understanding Emotional Flow: Recognize that emotions are meant to flow, not be stagnant. Emotions can become toxic when they're suppressed or denied.

2.Identifying Emotional Blockages: Learn to identify emotional blockages that hinder your well-being. These blockages may stem from past trauma or unresolved issues.

3.Expressing Emotions Safely: Discover healthy ways to express your emotions without harming yourself or others. Expression can be verbal, creative, or through physical activities.

4.Embracing Vulnerability: Understand that vulnerability is not weakness but a courageous act of opening up to yourself and others. It's a crucial step in emotional healing.

5.Healing Through Emotional Release: Recognize that allowing emotions to flow can be a form of self-healing. It's essential to let go of pent-up feelings to restore emotional well-being.

6.Seeking Support: Acknowledge that it's okay to seek professional help or lean on a support network when dealing with intense emotions. You don't have to navigate emotional challenges alone.

Self- Reflection Questions

1.Are you allowing your emotions to flow naturally, or do you tend to bottle them up?

_____

_____

_____

_____

_____

_____

_____

_____

2.What emotional blockages might be holding you back from living your most powerful life?

_____

_____

_____

_____

_____

_____

_____

_____

3.How do you currently express your emotions in a safe and constructive manner?

_____

_____

_____

_____

_____

_____

_____

_____

_____

4.How comfortable are you with being vulnerable
and sharing your true emotions with trusted
individuals?

_____

_____

_____

_____

_____

_____

_____

_____

_____

_____

5.Can you recall a time when allowing yourself to release emotions led to a sense of relief and healing?

_____

_____

_____

_____

_____

_____

_____

_____

_____

_____

6.Have you considered reaching out to a
therapist, counselor, or a trusted friend when you
face overwhelming emotions?

_____

_____

_____

_____

_____

_____

_____

_____

Good Ground and Your Most Powerful Life

Key Lessons

1.Cultivate Your Heart's Soil: Just as a garden thrives in good soil, your life flourishes when you nurture the soil of your heart.

2.Embrace Your Emotions:Emotions are not your enemies; they are tools for self-discovery and transformation.

3.Heal and Grow from Trauma:The process of healing from trauma can strengthen your body and create a foundation for a more powerful life.

4.Calm Anxiety Through Emotional Wellness: Cultivating emotional well-being can help calm anxiety and lead to a more peaceful mind.

5.Embracing your emotions can unlock a new level of spiritual power and connection in your life.

6.Nurture Your Heart's Potential: you are setting yourself free to live in alignment with your true purpose and potential.

Self-Reflection Questions

1.Are you actively tending to the emotional well-being of your heart, creating fertile ground for growth?

2.Are you open to fully experiencing and learning from your emotions, even the challenging ones?

_____

_____

_____

_____

_____

_____

_____

_____

3.Have you acknowledged and addressed past traumas, recognizing their impact on your emotional landscape?

_____

_____

_____

_____

_____

_____

_____

_____

_____

_____

4.How can you integrate emotional wellness
practices into your daily life to manage anxiety?

_____

_____

_____

_____

_____

_____

_____

_____

_____

_____

5. What spiritual practices resonate with you and support your journey toward emotional wholeness?

_____

_____

_____

_____

_____

_____

_____

_____

_____

6.What steps can you take to prioritize and
nurture your heart's potential for a more powerful
life?

Ground Zero

Key Lessons

1.Emotions Are Not Your Enemies:Emotions are not adversaries; they are valuable aspects of your human experience. Embrace them as allies in your journey towards personal growth.

2.Cultivate Emotional Awareness:Developing emotional awareness is essential. It allows you to understand and respond to your feelings effectively, leading to a more fulfilling life.

3.Healing Begins with Acknowledgment: The first step towards healing is acknowledging the emotional wounds or traumas you may be carrying. Avoiding or denying them can hinder your progress.

4.Accept Vulnerability: Accept vulnerability and authenticity can lead to emotional strength. It's okay to show your true self to yourself and others.

5.Nurture Your Emotional Soil: Create an environment within yourself that fosters emotional well-being and growth. Just as a garden needs care, your emotional landscape requires nurturing.

6.Seek Support and Guidance:Don't hesitate to seek support and guidance from professionals, friends, or mentors. They can provide valuable insights and help you navigate your emotional journey effectively.

Self-Reflection Questions

1 .Have you been viewing your emotions as adversaries rather than allies on your journey to self-discovery and personal growth?

_____

_____

_____

_____

_____

_____

_____

_____

2.Are you in touch with your emotions, or do you tend to suppress or ignore them? How can greater emotional awareness benefit your life?

_____

_____

_____

_____

_____

_____

_____

_____

_____

_____

3.Have you acknowledged the emotional wounds
or traumas you may be carrying? How can
acknowledging them be the first step toward
healing?

_____

_____

_____

_____

_____

_____

_____

_____

_____

_____

4.Are you open to being vulnerable and authentic with yourself and others, recognizing that vulnerability can lead to greater emotional strength?

_____

_____

_____

_____

_____

_____

_____

_____

_____

5. What steps can you take to create an environment within yourself that nurtures emotional well-being and growth, just like tending to a garden?

_____

_____

_____

_____

_____

_____

_____

6.Are you open to seeking support and guidance from professionals, friends, or mentors to help you navigate your emotional landscape and personal growth journey?

How Does Your Garden Grow?

Key Lessons

1.Guarding Your Emotions: Emotions are like seeds in your emotional garden. Just as a gardener tends to their plants, you must nurture your emotions with care and attention.

2.Soil of Self-Compassion: Your emotional soil needs self-compassion.

3.Embracing Vulnerability: Like tender shoots breaking through the soil, embracing vulnerability allows your authentic emotions to surface.

4.Patience and Growth: Gardens take time to flourish. Likewise, your emotional well-being is a journey that requires patience.

5.Weeding Out Negativity: Just as weeds can overtake a garden, negative emotions can overwhelm your emotional landscape.

6.Harvesting Joy: Just as gardens yield a bountiful harvest, your emotional garden can produce joy and fulfillment.

Self-Reflection Questions

1.Are you supporting your emotions like a gardener tends to their plants?

2.Is your emotional soil rich with self-compassion, providing a fertile ground for your emotions to thrive?

_____

_____

_____

_____

_____

_____

_____

_____

_____

3.Are you open to vulnerability, allowing your
authentic emotions to surface and grow?

_____

_____

_____

_____

_____

4.Do you actively identify and remove negativity from your emotional landscape, just as a gardener weeds out unwanted plants?

_____

_____

5.Are you patient with your emotional growth, understanding that it takes time for your emotional garden to flourish?

_____

_____

_____

_____

_____

_____

_____

_____

6.Are you prepared to harvest the joy and fulfillment that comes from supporting your emotions?

Water,Water Everywhere

Key Lessons

1.Emotions Are Like Water: Emotions, much like water, are fluid and constantly changing. They flow through your life, and it's essential to understand and navigate them rather than resist or suppress them.

2.Allowing Emotions to Flow: Just as a garden needs water to thrive, your emotional well-being depends on allowing your emotions to flow naturally. Resisting or damming up your feelings can lead to stagnation and emotional distress.

3.Balancing the Emotional Landscape: In gardening, the right balance of water is crucial. Similarly, in life, it's important to find a balance in how you respond to and express your emotions, avoiding extremes of emotional suppression or overwhelm.

4.Learning from Storms: Just as storms bring necessary rain to nourish the earth, emotional storms can be opportunities for growth and renewal. Reflect on how you can learn from challenging emotions and use them as catalysts for positive change.

5.Tending to Emotional Weeds: Like unwanted weeds in a garden, negative emotions can take root if not addressed. Consider how you can identify and manage negative emotions in your life to maintain emotional well-being.

6.Nurturing Emotional Soil: Just as fertile soil is essential for a healthy garden, the state of your emotional "soil" impacts your emotional well-being. Reflect on what you can do to nurture and create a positive emotional environment within yourself.

Self-Reflection Questions

1.Are you allowing your emotions to flow naturally, or are you resisting or suppressing them? How can you better embrace the fluidity of your emotions?

2. What is the current balance in your emotional landscape? Are you leaning towards emotional suppression or emotional overwhelm?

---

3. Think about a recent emotional "storm" or challenge in your life. What did you learn from it, and how did it contribute to your growth or renewal?

_____

_____

_____

_____

_____

_____

_____

_____

_____

_____

4.Are there any lingering negative emotions that
you've neglected, akin to unwanted weeds in a
garden? How can you address and manage these
emotions for your emotional well-being?

_____

_____

_____

_____

_____

_____

_____

_____

_____

5.Consider the state of your emotional "soil" the internal environment where your emotions take root. What can you do to nurture this soil for healthier emotional growth?

_____

_____

_____

_____

_____

_____

6.How can you apply the analogy of water and gardening to your own emotional journey? What insights can you gain from this comparison to better tend to your emotional well-being?

Dust of the Ground

Key Lessons

1.Embrace Your Origins: You are created from the dust of the ground, a beautiful and divine creation. Embrace your origin as a unique and precious being.

2.Recognize Your Fragility: Just as a garden requires care and protection, acknowledge your emotional fragility. Understand that it's okay to need nurturing and support.

3.Cultivate Self-Compassion:Extend the same care to yourself as you would to a garden. Practice self-compassion and gentleness when dealing with your emotions.

4.Nurture Your Emotional Soil:Like a garden, your emotional well-being depends on the quality of the soil (your heart). Invest in practices that nurture emotional wellness and growth.

5.Embrace Imperfection:Gardens aren't always perfect, and neither are you. Accept that growth involves imperfection and mistakes. Embrace your growth process.

6.Seek Growth and Transformation: Just as a garden grows and transforms over time, recognize that you have the capacity for growth and transformation, especially when it comes to your emotional life.

Self-Reflection Questions

1.Have you fully accepted and celebrated your unique origin and existence?

_____

_____

_____

_____

_____

_____

_____

_____

2.How well do you recognize and address your emotional vulnerabilities?

_____

_____

_____

_____

_____

_____

_____

_____

_____

_____

3.Are you as compassionate with yourself as you
are with others when you face emotional
challenges?

_____

_____

_____

_____

_____

_____

_____

_____

_____

_____

4. What practices can you implement to improve the "soil" of your heart and promote emotional well-being?

_____

_____

_____

_____

_____

_____

_____

5. How comfortable are you with embracing imperfections and learning from your mistakes?

_____

_____

_____

_____

_____

_____

_____

_____

_____

_____

6.What steps can you take to actively seek personal growth and transformation in your emotional journey?

_____

_____

_____

Shaky Ground

Key Lessons

1.Emotions as Messengers: Emotions are like messengers trying to convey important information about your inner world. They arise for a reason, and ignoring them can lead to internal turmoil.

2 The Impact of Suppression: Suppressing or dismissing your emotions can create a shaky foundation within yourself, causing anxiety and inner turmoil to persist.

3.Mind-Body Connection: The state of your emotions affects your physical well-being. Understanding and addressing emotional turmoil can lead to improved physical health.

4.Recognizing Emotional Patterns: Take time to recognize recurring emotional patterns in your life. These patterns can provide valuable insights into your inner landscape.

5.Acceptance and Healing: Accepting your emotions, even the uncomfortable ones, is a crucial step toward healing and emotional well-being.

6.Nurturing the Garden Within: Your emotional well-being is like tending to a garden within your heart. It requires ongoing care, attention, and cultivation to thrive and yield the fruits of a powerful life.

Self-Reflection Questions

1.Have you been treating your emotions as messengers, or have you been trying to suppress them? How can acknowledging their messages benefit you?

_____

_____

_____

_____

_____

_____

_____

_____

_____

2.Reflect on times when you felt a sense of inner turmoil. Could this turmoil be linked to the suppression or dismissal of certain emotions? What can you do to address this?

_____

_____

_____

_____

_____

_____

_____

_____

_____

3.How do you notice the connection between your emotional state and your physical well-being? Are there any patterns or symptoms you've observed?

_____

_____

_____

_____

_____

_____

_____

_____

_____

4.Take a moment to identify recurring emotional patterns in your life. What do these patterns reveal about your inner world and the areas that might need attention?

_____

_____

_____

_____

_____

_____

_____

_____

_____

5.Consider the idea that science is an ongoing
quest for knowledge and understanding. How
does this inspire you to explore and learn more
about the cosmos and other fields of science?

_____

_____

_____

_____

_____

_____

6.How have you been nurturing your emotional well-being lately? Are there specific practices or habits that contribute positively to the "garden" within your heart?

Wilderness

Key Lessons

1.Embrace the Wilderness: Your emotional journey may sometimes feel like a wilderness, but within it lies the potential for profound growth and self-discovery.

2.Facing Unresolved Emotions: The wilderness often confronts you with unresolved emotions and past traumas. Confronting these emotions is essential for healing and personal transformation.

3.Navigating Uncertainty: In the emotional wilderness, uncertainty is common. Learn to navigate this uncertainty with courage, trusting that it's a necessary part of your growth.

4.Seeking Guidance: Just as explorers in the wilderness seek guides, consider seeking guidance and support from therapists, mentors, or trusted individuals as you navigate your emotional landscape.

5.Resilience and Adaptability: The wilderness teaches adaptability and resilience. Emotions can be unpredictable, but you have the capacity to adapt and thrive even in challenging emotional terrain.

6.Discovering Hidden Strengths: Within the wilderness of emotions, you may uncover hidden strengths and resources that you didn't know you possessed. Embrace these newfound strengths as you journey within.

Self-Reflection Questions

1.Have you been avoiding or suppressing any unresolved emotions in your emotional wilderness, and how can facing them help you grow?

_____

_____

_____

_____

_____

_____

_____

_____

2.What uncertainties or challenges are currently present in your emotional landscape, and how can you embrace them as opportunities for growth?

_____

_____

_____

_____

_____

_____

_____

_____

_____

_____

3.Who can you turn to for guidance and support
as you navigate your emotional wilderness, and
how can their insights benefit your journey?

_____

_____

_____

_____

_____

_____

_____

_____

_____

_____

4.Reflect on a past experience where you demonstrated resilience and adaptability in the face of emotional challenges. How can you apply these qualities to your current emotional journey?

_____

_____

_____

_____

_____

_____

_____

_____

_____

5.What hidden strengths or resources have you
discovered within yourself during your
exploration of your emotional wilderness, and
how can you leverage them for personal growth?

_____

_____

_____

_____

_____

_____

_____

6.In what ways can you fully embrace the idea
that the wilderness of your emotions is a fertile
ground for your personal transformation and the
cultivation of your inner garden?

_____

_____

_____

_____

_____

_____

_____

_____

The Wisdom of Trees

Key Lessons

1.Rooted in Resilience: Emulate the strength and resilience of trees in facing life's challenges. Just as trees weather storms, you can overcome adversity.

2.Seasonal Growth: Recognize that personal growth occurs in seasons, much like the changing seasons of trees. Sometimes growth is visible, while other times it happens beneath the surface.

3.The Power of Deep Roots:Understand the importance of deep emotional roots for stability. Just as trees anchor themselves firmly, your emotional foundation can provide stability in turbulent times.

4.Shedding Old Leaves:Learn from trees that shed old leaves to make way for new growth. It's essential to let go of outdated beliefs and emotions to embrace personal transformation.

5.Providing Shelter and Nourishment: Recognize your capacity to provide shelter and nourishment to others, like the shade and sustenance trees offer to various creatures.

6.Connection to the Earth: Develop a deeper connection to the Earth, as trees do, to find spiritual grounding and a sense of belonging in the world.

Self-Reflection Questions

1.What challenges have you faced, and how have you demonstrated resilience in your life?

_____

_____

_____

_____

_____

_____

_____

_____

_____

_____

2.In which season of personal growth do you find yourself currently, and what aspects are you focusing on?

_____

_____

_____

_____

_____

_____

_____

_____

_____

3.How deep are your emotional roots, and what
practices can help you strengthen them?

_____

_____

_____

4.What old beliefs or habits are you ready to shed to make room for personal growth?

5.How can you be a source of support and
nourishment to those around you?

_____

_____

_____

_____

_____

_____

_____

_____

_____

6.How can you strengthen your connection to the
natural world to enhance your overall well-being
and sense of purpose?

_____

A Tree in the Temple

Key Lessons

1.Recognize Emotions as Sacred: Just as the tree in the temple is revered, your emotions should be treated as sacred and valuable. They have a purpose in your life.

2.Cultivate Emotional Awareness: Just as the temple needs constant care, you should cultivate awareness of your emotions. Pay attention to what they're telling you about yourself.

3.Release Judgment and Guilt: Just as the temple doesn't judge the tree's growth, you should release self-judgment and guilt about your emotions. They are a natural part of your inner landscape.

4.Prune Negative Emotions: Just as a gardener prunes a tree, you should learn to prune negative emotions that hinder your growth and well-being.

5.Nurture Positive Emotions: Just as a tree needs nourishment, nurture positive emotions that empower you and lead you toward a more powerful life.

6.Create a Sacred Emotional Space: Just as the temple provides a sacred space for the tree to flourish, create a sacred emotional space within yourself where your emotions can thrive and contribute to your well-being.

Self-Reflection Questions

1.How do you currently view your emotions? Are they sacred and valuable to you, or do you tend to dismiss or suppress them?

2.Are you actively cultivating emotional awareness in your life, paying attention to the messages your emotions are sending you?

3.Are you holding onto judgment and guilt regarding your emotional experiences? How might releasing these feelings benefit your emotional well-being?

_____

_____

_____

_____

_____

_____

_____

_____

_____

4.Which negative emotions are hindering your personal growth, and how can you begin to "prune" them from your life?

_____

_____

_____

_____

_____

_____

_____

_____

_____

5.What positive emotions do you need to nurture more intentionally to empower yourself and live a more powerful life?

_____

_____

_____

_____

_____

_____

6.Have you created a sacred emotional space within yourself where your emotions can thrive, or is this an area in which you need to invest more time and effort?

Healing the Broken Heart

Key Lessons

1.Acknowledging Pain:To heal a broken heart, you must first acknowledge the pain it holds.

2.Embracing Grief: Grief is a natural response to loss; allowing yourself to grieve is an essential step toward healing.

3.Seeking Support: Healing is often facilitated through connection with others; seek support and open up to trusted friends or professionals.

4.Forgiveness and Release:: Forgiveness, both for others and yourself, is a powerful tool for releasing emotional burdens.

5.Embracing Hope: Healing a broken heart is a process, and it's essential to hold onto hope for a brighter future.

6.Honoring Your Emotional Truth: It's essential to honor and express your authentic emotions rather than burying them to conform to external expectations.

Self- Reflection Questions

1.Have you been avoiding or suppressing emotional pain in your heart?

_____

_____

_____

_____

_____

_____

_____

_____

2.How have you been dealing with grief and loss in your life?

_____

_____

_____

_____

_____

_____

_____

_____

_____

_____

3.Have you been reaching out to others for support in your healing journey?

_____

_____

_____

_____

_____

_____

_____

_____

_____

_____

4.Are there individuals or situations that you need
to forgive in order to find emotional healing?

_____

_____

_____

_____

_____

_____

_____

_____

_____

5.How can you nurture hope and optimism as you work through your emotional pain?

6.Are there areas in your life where you've been suppressing your true emotions in order to meet others' expectations, and how can you begin to honor your emotional truth?

Self-Assessment Questions

1.Did you actively participate in the exercises and activities throughout the workbook? If not, what factors hindered your engagement, and how would you overcome them in the future?

_____

_____

_____

2.How effectively did you communicate your
thoughts, ideas, and solutions in the written
responses within the workbook?

_____

_____

_____

_____

_____

_____

_____

_____

_____

3.Were there any areas in the workbook where you felt uncertain or struggled to apply the concepts to your personal life? If so, how would you seek additional support or resources to address those challenges?

_____

_____

_____

_____

_____

_____

_____

_____

_____

4.How has completing this workbook impacted your overall understanding and approach to the topic? Can you identify any changes in your thoughts, behaviors, or attitudes?

_____

_____

_____

_____

_____

_____

_____

_____

_____

Made in the USA
Las Vegas, NV
07 April 2024

88310185R00056